The Pursuit of Excellence

The Story of a Lean Process Improvement

Professional

Copyrights © 2024

All Rights Reserved

Table of Contents

Chapter 1 How My Upbringing Set Me Up to Be an Agent of Change 1

Chapter 2 Understanding the Concept of Lean Process Improvement......7

Chapter 3 The Pitfalls of Neglecting Leadership and Cultural Change.....15

Chapter 4 Lessons from My Career: Successes and Failures.......................24

Chapter 5 Encouragement for LPI Professionals 35

Chapter 6 What's on the Horizon: Absolute Value Online Solutions.......45

Chapter 1
How My Upbringing Set Me Up to Be an Agent of Change

My journey to becoming a change agent began long before I entered the professional world. The foundation was laid during my formative years, shaped by experiences that instilled in me the values of patience, diversity, and the necessity of embracing change—principles that have guided my career as a Lean Process Improvement (LPI) professional.

Time and Reflection Heals All

My story begins with my adoption at just 13 months old, a pivotal moment that set the stage for my ability to adapt to change from a very young age. Five years later, my biological sister joined our family when she was six months old. Despite the complexities of our early lives, my sister and I became a tight-knit unit, bonded by an unspoken understanding of our unique circumstances.

My adoptive parents loved us deeply, and I have no doubt that they did their best to create a loving home for us. My mother, in particular, showered us with unconditional love, embracing her role as our protector and caretaker with fervor.

On the other hand, my father struggled to reconcile his love for my mother with the demands of a new family dynamic. Once filled with joy and companionship, their relationship gradually became strained under the weight of unspoken frustrations and unmet expectations.

As I witnessed the changes in my parents' relationship, I began to understand the complexities of human emotions and the impact of change on relationships. While rooted in love, my mother's protective nature sometimes felt overwhelming, and my father's attempts to express his feelings often came across as frustration and anger. Yet, as I grew older, I gained empathy for both, recognizing that although their actions and words toward each other and my sister and I may have felt harsh, unnecessary, or hurtful, at times, they ultimately originated from a place of love.

These early experiences taught me a valuable lesson: time can heal emotional wounds, and understanding the motivations behind people's actions is essential for fostering empathy and compassion. This understanding has been instrumental in my approach to LPI, where patience and empathy are critical for driving meaningful and lasting change.

Diversity is a Superpower

Growing up in Prince George's County, MD, with its predominantly Black population, offered me a unique perspective on diversity. Our community was a rarity in the

United States—a middle, upper-middle, and upper-class majority-Black community. My mother, with her roots in the Deep South during the Jim Crow and Civil Rights eras, was acutely aware of the challenges that Black people faced across the country. She made it a point to prepare us for a world that would not always be as welcoming as our hometown.

My mother emphasized the importance of personal character over skin color, teaching us that loyalty, morality, and integrity were the true measures of a person. She instilled in us the belief that we should not judge others based on their race but rather on their actions and values. This lesson was one of the most powerful gifts she gave me, teaching me to avoid stereotypes and appreciate the individuality of each person I encountered.

When it came time for me to choose a college, my mother encouraged me to attend Ohio University, a predominantly white institution. She knew that stepping out of my comfort zone would be challenging, but she also understood that exposure to different perspectives and environments would be crucial for my personal and professional growth. Many of my peers from high school struggled with the idea of leaving our community, and some returned home within a year if they even decided to leave in the first place. But my mother's wisdom in pushing me to embrace diversity paid off, as it helped me build the confidence to succeed in any environment.

This embrace of diversity has been a significant asset in my professional life. It has allowed me to approach LPI with a broader, more inclusive perspective, understanding that diverse teams bring creativity, adaptability, and innovation—essential ingredients for effective problem-solving and continuous improvement.

Change is Necessary for Reaching True Potential

Throughout my life, change has been a constant companion. From the shifts in my family dynamics to my move from a community where the vast majority of the population looked like me to a predominantly white university, these experiences ingrained in me the belief that change, though often uncomfortable, is a necessary catalyst for growth.

One of the most significant changes in my life occurred when I discovered my biological family, which included five additional siblings—two brothers and three sisters. This discovery was bittersweet, as I learned that my biological mother had struggled with addiction and had passed away from AIDS. Despite the emotional challenges of this revelation, my newfound family welcomed me with open arms, offering support, love, and answers to the questions I had carried for so long.

This experience, while deeply personal, underscored the importance of adaptability and resilience. At the same time that I was reconnecting with my biological family, my adoptive family was going through its own changes, including the loss of loved ones. These parallel events highlighted the inevitability of change and the need to embrace it with grace and open-mindedness.

In the realm of LPI, change is not just a process or a series of adjustments; it is the lifeblood of continuous improvement. My upbringing taught me that to unlock one's true potential, one must be willing to embrace and adapt to change. This principle is reflected in the core philosophy of LPI, where the pursuit of excellence requires a commitment to ongoing evolution.

Organizations that resist change risk being left behind as the world around them continues to evolve. Conversely, those who embrace change with a sense of urgency and purpose are more likely to achieve sustained success. My personal and professional experiences have shown me that change is not just inevitable—it is essential for growth, innovation, and long-term success.

My Upbringing Made Me a Change Agent

The lessons from my upbringing have profoundly influenced my approach to LPI. My early experiences with change, diversity, and personal growth have equipped me with a unique perspective on the complexities involved in driving change within organizations. These experiences have prepared me with the resilience, empathy, and adaptability needed to succeed as a LPI professional.

I hold no ill feelings toward anyone in my family. I love them deeply and know that they love me just the same. The challenges we faced together only strengthened my understanding of the human condition and the importance of empathy and patience in the face of change.

As an LPI professional, I have come to see that the principles that guided my personal growth are the same ones that drive successful organizational change. The pursuit of continuous improvement is not a one-time effort but a long-term commitment to excellence. It requires embracing change, fostering diversity, and cultivating a culture of empathy and collaboration.

My upbringing shaped me into the change agent I am today, and these experiences continue to inspire my work in my career. I believe that organizations can unlock their full potential through LPI's transformative power.

Chapter 2
Understanding the Concept of Lean Process Improvement

Process LPI is far more than a collection of techniques; it represents a transformative philosophy that can revolutionize industries. Originally developed within manufacturing, LPI aims to meet customer expectations and boost efficiency by eliminating waste. These principles evolved from Henry Ford's groundbreaking assembly line innovations and were later expanded upon by the advanced change leadership and continuous improvement methods implemented by Toyota.

The Origins of Lean Process Improvement

The LPI concept began in the 20th century with Henry Ford's assembly line, which marked a significant shift from batch production to continuous production. Seeing how successful this approach was, other manufacturers were inspired to explore similar efficiencies.

However, it was Toyota's work that truly defined what we know today as Lean practices. Toyota didn't just adopt these principles; they refined and expanded them through the Toyota Production System (TPS). Their focus on continuous improvement, waste reduction, quality enhancement, and delivering customer value really solidified the core ideas of LPI for me.

Most people spend more time and energy going around problems than trying to solve them.
Henry Ford

As I delved deeper into Lean principles, I noticed that their benefits were becoming increasingly apparent. Organizations across various industries began adapting these methods to tackle broader and more complex challenges. This evolution caught my attention when Lean started merging with Six Sigma, a methodology developed by Motorola in the 1980s. Six Sigma's focus on improving quality by reducing process variation through critical statistical analysis complemented Lean's emphasis on waste reduction.

When these two approaches combined, they formed Lean Six Sigma—a robust framework that I found to be incredibly effective for process improvement. This integrated approach not only tackles efficiency but also enhances quality, proving to be a powerful tool for organizations looking to elevate their operations.

"The most dangerous kind of waste is the waste we do not recognize."
Shigeo Shingo

The Versatility of Lean Process Improvement

One of the most significant attributes of LPI, in my view, is its adaptability. Although Lean was originally developed for manufacturing, I've discovered that its principles are highly applicable across a broad spectrum of industries. This adaptability arises from Lean's fundamental emphasis on eliminating process waste—a principle that is universally applicable to any industry where a product or service is delivered through a series of tasks, activities, or processes. Wherever information, materials, or people are required to pass through multiple departments or individuals to produce or deliver a final product or service, you can be certain that various forms of waste present themselves throughout the process. Whether its healthcare, finance, or any other field, the principles of Lean can be effectively utilized to streamline operations and enhance efficiency. Of all the 8 types of waste:

- Defects/Errors
- Overproduction
- Waiting
- Unused talent
- Transportation
- Inventory
- Motion

- Extra-Processing

At least one occurs in almost every industry, no matter what you produce or provide. Suppose the occurrence of any of these wastes has the potential to impact business performance metrics, such as sales, revenues, product or service quality, on-time delivery, safety, employee satisfaction, customer satisfaction, and/or brand reputation. In that case, your business needs LPI.

> *"There exist limitless opportunities in every industry. Where there is an open mind, there will always be a frontier."*
> Charles F. Kettering

The Transformative Power of Lean Process Improvement

In the healthcare sector, for instance, I've seen firsthand how LPI has been used to make a real difference. By applying Lean methodologies, I've observed improvements in various areas: operations are streamlined, patient waiting times are reduced, and patient access is enhanced. Additionally, Lean has contributed to a decrease in hospital-acquired infections and a reduction in healthcare costs. Through these methods, healthcare providers can create more efficient workflows, improve the overall quality of care, and deliver better outcomes for patients.

Similarly, I've noticed that the financial services industry has eagerly embraced LPI to tackle complex processes such as transactions, compliance, and customer service. Banks and financial institutions have leveraged these Lean principles to minimize the chances of errors, enhance service delivery, and boost overall efficiency. Techniques like value stream mapping and process standardization play a crucial role in helping these organizations streamline their operations and improve performance.

Customer service is another area where LPI can yield substantial benefits. In my experience, organizations that place a high priority on customer satisfaction utilize these Lean principles to enhance their service delivery and address customer issues more effectively. By focusing on eliminating waste, companies are able to provide superior quality and service to their customers. This approach not only improves the customer experience but also fosters greater loyalty and satisfaction, as clients feel valued and well-served.

LPI tools, such as root cause analyses, value stream mapping, 5S, visual management/control, pull systems, standardized work, and many others, are invaluable in helping organizations across various industries. I've found that these tools assist in identifying and permanently addressing pain points, leading to more efficient and effective operations. By implementing these Lean techniques, organizations can streamline processes, reduce waste, and enhance overall performance, making a significant impact on their operational efficiency.

A corporation is a living organism; it has to continue to shed its skin. Methods have to change. Focus has to change. Values have to change. The total of those changes is transformation.
Andrew Grove

LPI embodies a philosophy that encourages organizations to pursue excellence continuously. From my perspective, it promotes a mindset where processes are seen as dynamic and evolving, rather than static and fixed. This perspective helps foster a culture of continuous improvement, where every team member is encouraged to contribute ideas and actively seek ways to enhance both efficiency and quality. Embracing this mindset ensures that the pursuit of excellence is ongoing and that improvements are continually made.

"We cannot become what we want to be by remaining what we are."
Max DePree, Herman Miller

A customer-centric approach lies at the heart of LPI. From my perspective, by aligning processes with the needs and expectations of customers and consumers, organizations can deliver more meaningful and impactful outcomes. Lean's comprehensive view of process improvement looks at every aspect of an organization, striving to optimize all operations to achieve greater efficiency and effectiveness. This focus ensures that improvements not only enhance internal processes but also deliver value that resonates with customers.

Implementing LPI demands a strong commitment to change and a willingness to adopt new working methods. From my experience, it's crucial for organizations to engage their entire workforce and foster a culture of collaboration and continuous learning. Successful implementation starts with a thorough understanding of current processes, mapping them out to pinpoint areas of waste and inefficiency, and then making targeted improvements. LPI is centered on eliminating waste and enhancing value, with the goal of integrating these principles deeply into the organization's core operating system.

LPI is not just a set of practices but a transformative philosophy with the potential to profoundly impact a wide range of industries. From its manufacturing origins, Lean's principles offer a comprehensive framework for optimizing processes that extends far beyond the factory floor. I've seen how Lean has been effectively applied in sectors like healthcare, finance, customer service, and many others. By fostering a culture of continuous improvement and aligning operations with customer needs, organizations can achieve remarkable enhancements in both efficiency and quality. As LPI continues to evolve and adapt to new challenges, its potential to revolutionize industries remains vast and largely untapped.

"Perfection is not attainable. But if we chase perfection, we can catch excellence."

— Vince Lombardi is an American football player, coach, and executive.

Chapter 3
The Pitfalls of Neglecting Leadership and Cultural Change

In many organizations, I've observed that the potential of LPI remains untapped, often due to an insufficient emphasis on leadership and cultural change. Many organizations enter into LPI with high hopes of achieving transformative success. However, these efforts frequently fall short or are not sustained because they overlook critical elements essential for the success of LPI. A primary reason behind this failure often lies in a lack of genuine commitment from leadership. Executives, managers, supervisors, and front-line leaders sometimes perceive LPI methods as superficial changes that can be mandated rather than exemplified. These misconceptions lead to LPI never truly permeating the operating system of the organization, preventing it from achieving its full potential.

"Leadership is the art of giving people a platform for spreading ideas that work." —

Seth Godin

Most organizations that decide to embark on LPI often make the common initial mistake of bringing in one or several LPI professionals, such as myself. These individuals might be Continuous Improvement or Operational Excellence VPs, Directors, Managers, Specialists, or Consultants. Once these Lean professionals are onboarded, there's a tendency for operational leaders to expect them to lead the entire organization to the promised land of world-class operational excellence, as if they are messiahs fulfilling a long-awaited prophecy.

What operational leaders frequently overlook is that while LPI professionals are indeed Improvement Leaders, their role is not to single-handedly transform the organization. Instead, they are there to teach, guide, facilitate, and mentor the organization through the process of process improvement. Their responsibility is to help gain buy-in and build consensus on how to approach and apply process improvement methods, tactics, and strategies. They are not there to persuade the organization of the need for change—that is the crucial role of the operational leaders themselves.

"If you always do what you always did, you'll always get what you've always got."

– Henry Ford, Ford Motor Company

Often, LPI professionals find themselves unfairly blamed for not advancing the organization along the Lean journey at a satisfactory pace. In reality, the root cause of stagnation is frequently that the organization lacks a culture that accepts, understands, or embraces change. The challenge for LPI professionals is that they are not in charge of implementing this cultural shift. They are frequently given the title of "leader without authority," which means they are expected to hold people accountable without having direct means to enforce accountability.

All it takes is one instance where an individual fails to adhere to the required improvements, and if their Manager or Supervisor decides not to hold them accountable—for whatever reason—the LPI professional is powerless to effect change. Even a single occurrence of managerial or supervisory lack of dedication, ownership, or belief in the improvement effort can undermine the entire process. While many LPI professionals persevere, adapt, and manage to secure occasional wins, the organization seldom reaches a state of true operational excellence under these conditions.

For LPI to genuinely penetrate an organization's operating system and achieve lasting success, operational leaders must actively engage in and manage cultural change. They need to ensure that the organization comprehends that change is not only necessary but expected to secure its future.

So, what does it look like when an organization relies on LPI professionals to lead cultural change while absolving operational leaders of the responsibility?

1.) Work areas or departments are consistently solving the same problem over and over and over again
2.) There is a revolving door of LPI professional turnover
3.) LPI professionals are treated as overseers of a process or department. LPI professionals are often times asked to answer critical questions about the department or work area's operational performance instead of the operational leader.
4.) Process improvement initiatives deemed complete fail to sustain or continue to improve.
5.) The decision to take on an improvement initiative is frequently negotiated with managers, supervisors, and/or specialized skill staff members.
6.) Improvement projects are consistently put on hold or progress with no sense of urgency
7.) Operational leaders have the Just-Do-It mentality. LPI is not something you do…it is something you live.
8.) Operational or Department leaders look to the LPI professional for all the answers instead of engaging in the process improvement initiatives, learning as the

team learns, and participating in developing creative solutions with the people doing the work.

9.) LPI professionals are subordinate to operational leaders with conflicting priorities that do not understand what is required of them to create and sustain cultural change. These operational leaders usually see improvement initiatives as a hindrance to getting the job done.

10.) Organizations that have been engaged in LPI for more than five years and only a few "islands of excellence" (maybe) to show for their efforts. You can easily see and feel the effective integration of LPI by just walking through the facility.

The term "buy-in" is often used to explain why LPI professionals or projects fail to achieve their desired outcomes. While a lack of buy-in can be an issue with specific Lean methods or actions, it doesn't fully address why some organizations struggle to shift from simply doing LPI to truly living it. I've found that this represents a deeper issue than mere agreement.

True commitment goes beyond verbal endorsement. It requires active engagement and a fundamental shift in organizational culture to embrace change. In my experience, effective LPI implementation demands that operational leaders not only support change but are deeply involved in driving and communicating it. These leaders need to actively champion LPI initiatives, ensuring that the evolving mindset is not just endorsed but deeply embedded within the organization's practices and ethos. For LPI to truly take root and succeed, it has to become an integral part of the organization, driven by leaders who are committed to fostering and sustaining that change.

I believe that operational leadership commitment is crucial for the success of LPI because it directly influences how change is perceived and executed within the organization. Leaders who view LPI as just a passing trend or a set of superficial tactics are unlikely to invest the necessary time and resources for meaningful improvement. Instead, they might apply minimal effort and fail to address the deeper cultural changes required to support LPI effectively. This lack of commitment can lead to projects being implemented half-heartedly, resulting in initiatives that lack the support and momentum needed to effect real and lasting change.

Moreover, I've found that failing to prioritize cultural change can significantly undermine the effectiveness of LPI initiatives. For LPI to be successful, it must be interlaced into the fabric of the organization's daily operations and values. This requires a cultural transformation where continuous improvement becomes a core aspect of the organization's functions. Operational leaders play a pivotal role in fostering this culture. They must set an example by embracing LPI principles and demonstrating their commitment through actions and decisions. This involves more than just endorsing LPI; it means actively participating in and promoting the changes that LPI entails.

"Leadership is not magnetic personality, that can just as well be a glib tongue. It is not 'making friends and influencing people' that is flattery. Leadership is lifting a person's vision to higher sights, the raising of a person's performance to a higher standard, the building of a personality beyond its normal limitations." —

Peter F. Drucker

Operational leaders must be the driving force behind creating a culture that embraces continuous improvement. From my perspective, this culture should be marked by openness to change, a willingness to experiment, and a focus on learning from mistakes. Leaders need to foster an environment where these values are not only encouraged but also expected as the norm. This cultural shift is essential for ensuring that LPI efforts are sustained over time and that improvements are continually pursued. Without this transformation, LPI initiatives may struggle to gain traction and achieve the intended results.

The lack of a supportive culture also challenges the maintenance of momentum for LPI projects. From my perspective, when leadership does not actively champion the changes required by LPI, employees may view these initiatives as temporary or insincere. This can result in a lack of enthusiasm and engagement from the workforce, further delaying the success of the projects. Employees need to see that their leaders are genuinely committed to the principles of LPI and that these principles are being integrated into everyday practices. When leadership fails to provide this support, it can create a disconnect between the goals of LPI and the reality of organizational operations.

"Change will not come if we wait for some other person or some other time. We are the ones we've been waiting for. We are the change that we seek." —

Barack Obama

Furthermore, I've found that successful LPI initiatives necessitate leaders who not only support change but also hold teams accountable for both implementing and sustaining these changes. Accountability is a critical element of LPI, as it ensures that everyone in the organization remains aligned with the goals of the improvement efforts. Leaders must set clear expectations, monitor progress, and address any obstacles.

Without this level of accountability, LPI projects can lose focus and fail to deliver the desired outcomes.

"Responsibility equals accountability equals ownership, and sense of ownership is most powerful weapon a team of an organization can have"-

— Pat Summitt

Leaders must also recognize that cultural change is a gradual process that requires persistent effort. Transforming organizational culture is not something that happens overnight. From my experience, it involves ongoing communication, consistent reinforcement of new behaviors, and actively addressing resistance to change. Operational leaders must be prepared for this long-term commitment and willing to invest the necessary time and resources. This commitment is crucial for ensuring that LPI initiatives are not temporary fixes but lead to sustained improvements.

"Change before you have to."

- Jack Welch1

Chapter 4

Lessons from My Career: Successes and Failures

Reflecting on my career, I've had the opportunity to experience both the triumphs and the trials of LPI implementation. These experiences have provided me with invaluable insights into what makes LPI integration successful and what causes it to falter. My career has been a tale of two sides of the same coin. In the first half, I witnessed organizations achieve remarkable success through well-executed LPI strategies. In the latter half, I observed organizations struggle to gain traction, offering a stark contrast and shaping my understanding of LPI's complexities.

After graduating from Ohio University in 2002 with a Bachelor of Science in Industrial Engineering Technology, I began my professional journey at Trim Systems, now known as Commercial Vehicle Group (CVG). At the time, CVG primarily supplied interior systems to the commercial heavy-duty trucking industry. CVG has since expanded into diverse sectors, such as e-commerce, transportation, warehousing, and construction equipment. I do not doubt that CVG's commitment to LPI has played a significant role in propelling this growth.

My first role was as a production supervisor, an exciting and daunting position for someone fresh out of college. With little experience managing people and operations—especially those older and more seasoned than myself—I approached the job with a blend of eagerness and humility. I quickly realized that leading effectively meant learning not only from my superiors but also from my subordinates. This approach helped me build strong relationships and gain respect, which became crucial when CVG rolled out its Total Quality Production System (TQPS) program.

TQPS was a homegrown, week-long interactive LPI workshop, part of CVG's initiative to educate all operations employees in Lean principles. Initially, I was skeptical about the effectiveness of these Lean methods. However, I started to see tangible improvements after immersing myself in the TQPS program and applying simple and intermediate LPI tools like 5S, visual management, and line balancing. We began to reduce defects, complete our work without overtime, and eliminate the need for exhausting campaigns to separate good and defective products. The most significant change was that my team began to operate autonomously, producing consistent results and recognizing when the process was not functioning as it should before major issues arose.

Six months after the launch of TQPS, CVG introduced an operations role called TQPS Coordinator, which was a promotion from my production supervisor position. I was offered the position, and my journey as a LPI professional had truly begun. In addition to conducting TQPS workshops at the Chillicothe, OH plant, I was tasked with spreading TQPS or LPI through the facility via TQPS Cell Certification. This certification involved collaborating with operational teams in various product production cells to implement a production system measured by quantifiable metrics related to quality, safety, productivity, employee engagement, and LPI understanding and application.

My authority in this role was solidified by my prior success as a production supervisor, where I had already gained respect as an operational leader. Over the next year, TQPS spread like wildfire throughout the plant, and both CVG and its customers reaped the benefits. Unbeknownst to me then, this approach—starting with an operational leader who found success using LPI, promoting them, and then tasking them with spreading LPI throughout the organization—was replicated in other CVG plants. This strategic approach was key to CVG's long-term success in LPI implementation, which I am confident continues to drive their operations today.

In August 2006, I transitioned to a Continuous Improvement Strategic Business Unit Manager role at Sullair

Corporation in Michigan City, IN. Sullair, a manufacturer of rotary screw industrial and construction air compressors, was owned by Hamilton Sundstrand, a subsidiary of United Technologies (UTC). My time at Sullair was the most educational and rewarding experience of my career, providing me with a deep understanding of how a structured LPI program like UTC's Achieving Competitive Excellence (ACE) could transform an organization.

ACE was a rigorous LPI program with advancement levels—qualifying, bronze, silver, and gold—each requiring specific criteria in business operational performance, Lean methodology education, application, and execution. At the time of my hiring, Sullair's Unit/OEM division had slipped from ACE Silver to Bronze status, and I was brought in to help restore its standing.

At Sullair, I was in a leadership role without direct authority, which could have been challenging if UTC had not implemented an effective top-down communication strategy. UTC's leadership consistently emphasized that ACE was the operating system for all UTC-owned companies. This message resonated from the top to the bottom of every subsidiary, including Sullair. Sullair's president, vice president, business unit managers, and operations leaders reinforced this message in every meeting and staff address, making it clear that ACE was not just another initiative—it was how we did business.

This unwavering commitment to ACE from all levels of leadership created an environment where there was no need to convince teams to buy into the program; it was thoroughly ingrained in the organizational culture. Supervisors and operations leaders actively sought out ACE Business Unit Managers like myself for assistance with education and implementation. This culture of accountability and support was instrumental in our success.

By December 2008, the Unit/OEM division had regained its ACE Silver status and undergone a profound transformation. The plant looked and operated differently due to the effective use of visual management and 5S techniques. We transitioned from batch machining and assembly processes to self-contained product family-based value streams, realizing millions of dollars in inventory reduction through effective kanban and pull systems. Additionally, we saw massive improvements in on-time delivery and significant reductions in defect escapes to our customers. Sullair lived and breathed ACE, which showed in every aspect of the operation.

Unfortunately, in late 2009, I was laid off from Sullair due to the economic downturn, which was a tough time for American manufacturers. Despite this, I feel blessed to have been part of such an amazing transformation and have played an integral role in making it happen. My time at Sullair left an indelible mark on my career, reinforcing the importance of a unified, top-down commitment to LPI.

After Sullair, I took on a 2nd shift production supervisor role at Agrana Fruit US in Botkins, OH, a manufacturer of custom-developed pasteurized fruit preparations for the dairy industry. While Agrana did not have a formal LPI program, they knew of the methodology and were excited to have someone with my experience on board. Back in a position of operational authority, I used that authority to introduce my crew to LPI concepts like root cause analysis to reduce ingredient addition errors, setup reduction, and Pareto analysis to minimize sanitation times and reduce equipment downtime. My time at Agrana was short but reaffirmed how quickly and effectively LPI can be adopted when supported by operational leaders.

In 2012, I joined Wabash National, a standard and customized commercial trailer manufacturer, as an Operational Excellence (OpEx) Specialist. This role initially appeared to offer the opportunity to build something akin to UTC's ACE program. My early work at Wabash included developing an LPI simulation workshop using Legos and reducing cycle times in key production processes by as much as 50%. We identified 84 kaizen events across the two main trailer production lines, which accounted for 90% of Wabash's 2012 production volume. The future seemed bright, and Wabash was primed for an LPI explosion.

However, despite these early successes, Wabash struggled with organizational alignment and cultural change. The OpEx department was eventually broken up, with each specialist placed under different plant managers. While some of these managers were supportive, many were traditional manufacturing leaders focused on production at any cost. They saw LPI as a separate function rather than an integral part of their operations. This fragmentation resulted from the Executive Leadership team's focus on growth through acquisitions and market expansion rather than prioritizing organic growth through cultural transformation and process improvement. While entering new markets and acquiring organizations are critical CEO responsibilities, significant risks emerge when flawed processes, entrenched habits, and a stagnant culture are carried into these new ventures. Ultimately, if you continue to operate as you always have, you'll achieve the same results—poor processes inevitably produce poor outcomes, especially when striving for innovation. This lack of emphasis on organic growth led to missed opportunities and the underutilization of OpEx specialists.

One of my proudest achievements at Wabash was a project in a small sub-assembly area that assembled trailer landing gear. This project was a textbook example of LPI application that resulted in a 75% reduction in finished goods, a 50% reduction in material travel, a 30% reduction in operator travel, a 30% labor reallocation, a 50% floor space reduction, and a 95% reduction in wrong landing gear installs on trailer lines. Despite these impressive results, the project was not leveraged as a catalyst for broader cultural change. Wabash's inability to capitalize on these wins was a stark reminder that believing in LPI and wanting problems solved are not the same. Wabash's executive leadership was so focused on production that they did not even realize we had achieved such an outstanding accomplishment. It was a stark reminder that without a unified, top-down commitment to change, even the most successful projects can fail to create lasting impact.

Following my time at Wabash, I joined C&D Technologies in Attica, IN, as Plant Quality Manager. C&D, a lead-acid backup power manufacturer, was another organization where LPI struggled to take root. Despite some successes in improving the quality management system and manufacturing yield, the company's resistance to change and lack of support for LPI initiatives made it clear that a cultural shift was needed before meaningful progress could be made. Engineers were extremely attached to the products and processes they developed, the lone LPI professional on staff had zero authority and was completely underutilized, and an undercurrent of acceptance of unethical behavior permeated the organization's leadership culture. All these circumstances made it impossible to foster a culture of continuous improvement. Toward the end of my time at C&D, the company was purchased by a venture capital firm whose primary focus was cleaning up and selling the business. While these new owners were intelligent businessmen, they knew little about the power of LPI beyond a quality improvement tool known as PFMEA. They successfully cleansed the organization of unethical practices but were far from creating a culture ready to embrace LPI.

In 2020, I joined IU Health as an Operational Excellence Leader, which I have found to be the most fulfilling role of my career. However, healthcare, in general, presents its own unique challenges to LPI integration. The industry's understandable focus on patient care and empathy towards the extenuating circumstances patients may go through can make it difficult for operational leaders and clinical staff to see the value in applying Lean methodologies, which are often associated with manufacturing. Additionally, the influence of specialized clinical staff, such as doctors and advanced practice providers, on operations can create barriers to process improvement. I was incredibly surprised to learn that the goals and objectives of specialized clinical staff don't always align with the goals and objectives of the healthcare system. That being said, I feel the more significant issue is we currently have a healthcare system plagued by a web of complications fueled by insurance and pharmaceutical corporation greed, coupled with political agendas. The healthcare system faces significant challenges on these fronts that not only hinder the affordability of care but also compromise its ability to operate efficiently and effectively. This has led to limited access to health care and negative outcomes for many individuals. These complex issues demand the transformative power of Lean Process Improvement to drive meaningful change.

Despite these challenges, I believe the healthcare industry is slowly coming around to the benefits of LPI. As more examples of successful LPI applications emerge, I am confident that healthcare will embrace Lean principles more fully, giving LPI a chance to have a more robust effect on creating better patient outcomes, reducing healthcare costs, and improving access to healthcare.

The successes and failures I've experienced throughout my career have taught me that LPI is not just a set of tools or methodologies—it's a cultural transformation that requires commitment from every level of an organization. Effective LPI integration depends on strong leadership, a unified vision, and the willingness to embrace change. While the journey is often challenging, the rewards of creating a culture of continuous improvement are well worth the effort.

As I continue my work at IU Health, I remain dedicated to the principles of LPI and look forward to spreading the word about it. I hope that more organizations will take the leap of faith and unlock their full potential through these transformative practices.

Chapter 5

Encouragement for LPI Professionals

To all LPI professionals working worldwide, your role is pivotal and challenging in pursuing continuous improvement within organizations. The journey you undertake is fraught with obstacles, but the impact of your efforts can be truly transformative. I want to offer some words of encouragement and practical advice to help you navigate the complexities of your role effectively.

The path of a LPI professional is often filled with difficulties and challenges. One of the most common hurdles I've faced is resistance to change. It can be disheartening to encounter pushback from those who are reluctant to embrace new methods or processes. But understand this: resistance is as much a part of the process as change itself. Human nature inherently resists the unknown, and any effort to alter the status quo can be met with anxiety and apprehension. Developing a thick skin is essential. You must remind yourself that while change is a constant in organizations, resistance is equally a constant in human behavior.

As LPI professionals, we must recognize that the success of our efforts depends not only on our expertise in Lean methodologies but also on our understanding of human psychology. From my experience, it's equally important to learn what turns people off and what motivates them. Understanding the psychological triggers that influence behavior is crucial for effectively engaging your audience and driving change. You must learn the language and communication styles that resonate with different individuals and teams, meeting people where they are rather than where you expect them to be. By tailoring your approach to your audience's unique needs and attitudes, you can reduce resistance and increase the likelihood of successful implementation.

Building and nurturing organizational relationships is another critical aspect of your role. Establishing trust with colleagues, leaders, and team members can significantly ease the process of change. People are more likely to engage with and support LPI initiatives when they trust the individual leading the change. This trust is built through consistent actions, understanding, and empathy. You must actively work to understand the perspectives and concerns of those involved and demonstrate genuine respect for their viewpoints.

Your ability to connect with people on a human level is just as important as your technical skills. This is where your knowledge of psychology becomes invaluable. By understanding what motivates people, you can communicate in ways that foster trust and cooperation. For example, some people may respond well to data-driven arguments, while others might be more motivated by stories of how change has positively impacted others. By tailoring your communication to meet the needs of your audience, you create an environment where collaboration is encouraged, and the path to improvement becomes smoother.

As an LPI professional, your role in the process of process improvement is to provide guidance and facilitate improvement, not to provide all the answers. It's important to remember that the solutions to many problems will come from within the teams you are working with. Your role is to provide the support and direction required by these teams in the process of developing and implementing solutions. You are also responsible for motivating team members to take ownership of the problem-solving process while you act as a resource and mentor. This approach empowers individuals and helps build their capacity for continuous improvement, creating a self-sustaining and resilient organization.

Understanding the psychology of team dynamics is crucial in this aspect. People need to feel that they are a part of the solution, not just passive recipients of change. Encourage open dialogue, actively listen to concerns, and acknowledge the emotional aspects of change. By doing so, you empower teams to take responsibility for their improvement processes, leading to more sustainable and meaningful change.

When dealing with issues that span multiple departments, bringing everyone together to address the challenges is crucial. Multi-departmental problems require a collective effort to resolve, as each department will have its own concerns and require solutions accordingly. Organize meetings or workshops where representatives from all affected departments can share their perspectives and work collaboratively towards common goals. This inclusive approach ensures that all voices are heard and that solutions are comprehensive and considerate of the needs of each department. By facilitating open communication and collaboration, you help to break down silos and promote a unified approach to improvement.

Change is inherently a gradual process, and patience is a key virtue for LPI professionals. It is important to recognize that meaningful improvements take time to achieve. The resistance and inertia you encounter may not be overcome overnight. Persistence and a long-term perspective are necessary for driving successful LPI initiatives. Keep in mind that each small step forward contributes to the overall goal, and progress, even if slow, it's still progress.

Your understanding of human psychology will serve you well here. Change is often an emotional process as much as it is a rational one. People need time to adjust to new ideas and processes. Being patient and empathetic, acknowledging their fears and concerns, and providing reassurance will go a long way in easing the transition. The more you can connect with people emotionally, the more successful you will be in guiding them through the change process.

One of the more challenging aspects I found in LPI work is obtaining reliable data. Data is critical for informed decision-making, yet it can often be difficult to collect, analyze, and trust. Avoid the trap of over-analysis, which can lead to paralysis by analysis. Use the data you have to make informed decisions and drive improvements, even if it's not perfect. As you implement changes and gather more data, the quality and reliability of your information will improve. Focus on making incremental improvements based on the best available data and refine your processes as you go along.

Seasoned LPI professionals are a rare breed. Improvement professionals often see more failure than success, and because we are guiding the process of process improvement, we often don't even get credit for the successes. But that does not diminish the value of the work we do. In fact, it highlights the resilience and dedication required to be successful in this field.

Here are some tips that have helped me throughout my career:

Develop a Thick Skin: As I mentioned earlier, you will face resistance, and sometimes that resistance will be personal. People who are against change or don't want to take on the burden of execution may lie about you or tell your boss all kinds of things to discredit you. Remember, telling people they need to change can invoke strong emotions, and when people act out of emotion, they may say and do anything. Don't take it personally—stay focused on your mission.

Study Human Psychology: Beyond mastering Lean methodologies, invest time in understanding human behavior. Learn what turns people on and off, and adapt your communication style to engage your audience effectively. This knowledge will help you navigate resistance, build trust, and lead change more successfully.

Build and Nurture Relationships: Trust is your most valuable asset. Do what you say you are going to do, and make a point to see and interact with those doing the work. Your job is a lot easier when people trust you and believe in your commitment to their success.

Guide, Don't Solve: Remember that you are there to guide the improvement process, not to come up with all the solutions. Don't let people rope you into thinking you have to have all the answers. The individuals on the front lines are often the best source of solutions. Your role is to show them what is wrong and teach them methods for improvement.

Facilitate Cross-Departmental Collaboration: When dealing with problems involving multiple people or departments, get everyone in the same room. Let them share what they go through to accomplish a common goal. This approach fosters understanding and leads to more effective, comprehensive solutions.

Be Patient: Organizational change is a slow and often painful process. Don't get discouraged if progress seems minimal or slow. Every small victory contributes to the larger goal.

Trust Your Data (Eventually): Getting data you trust will always be an issue. Avoid paralysis by analysis. Once you have some data you can reasonably trust, move forward. As the process improves, so will the quality of your data.

Embrace Continuous Learning: Lean is not a static discipline; it evolves. Stay updated with the latest trends, tools, and methodologies in Lean and continuous improvement. Attend workshops, read books, and participate in professional networks to continuously expand your knowledge and skills.

Practice Active Listening. One of the most powerful tools in your toolkit is the ability to listen actively. Understand the concerns, ideas, and feedback of those you work with. By truly hearing what others say, you can better address their needs and gain their trust.

Be Adaptable: Every organization and team are different. What works in one setting may not work in another. Be ready to adapt your approach to fit the specific culture, goals, and challenges of the organization you are working with. Flexibility is key to finding the best solutions.

Celebrate Small Wins: Recognize and celebrate even the smallest victories in the improvement process. Acknowledging progress, no matter how minor, boosts morale and encourages continued effort. It also helps to keep the momentum going, especially in long-term projects.

Develop a Strong Business Acumen: Understanding the broader business context in which you are working is crucial. Learn about the organization's financial, operational, and strategic aspects. This knowledge will help you align Lean initiatives with the organization's overall goals and demonstrate the value of your work in business terms.

Leverage Data Visualization: Use data visualization tools to make complex data more accessible and understandable to stakeholders. Visual tools like dashboards, charts, and graphs can help communicate the impact of Lean initiatives more effectively and foster better decision-making.

Focus on Root Cause Analysis: Always dig deeper into problems to identify their root causes rather than just addressing symptoms. Techniques like the 5 Whys or Fishbone

Diagram can help you and your team reach the core of issues, leading to more sustainable solutions.

Build a Cross-Functional Skill Set: Expand your expertise beyond just Lean tools. Understanding other areas like project management, change management, and organizational behavior can make you a more well-rounded professional and increase your ability to lead complex improvement projects.

Encourage a Culture of Continuous Improvement: Work to create an environment where continuous improvement is part of the organizational culture. Encourage team members to always look for ways to improve processes, no matter how small. This culture shift can lead to sustained long-term improvements.

As you continue your journey as an LPI professional, remember that your work has far-reaching implications. You are improving processes and building more efficient, effective, and resilient organizations. The challenges you face are significant, but so are the rewards. Each improvement you facilitate, no matter how small, contributes to a larger goal of continuous improvement and operational excellence.

Your role is crucial in helping organizations navigate the complexities of change. Stay focused, stay resilient, and continue to be the driving force behind positive transformation. The journey may be long and challenging, but the impact of your work is undeniable.

Understanding and applying Lean methodologies are essential, but your ability to connect with people, understand their motivations, and guide them through change with empathy and insight is equally important. The more you combine your technical skills with a deep understanding of human psychology, the more effective you will be in your role.

As you reflect on your role, remember that you are not alone. There is a global community of LPI professionals who share your challenges, your frustrations, and your victories. Together, we are all part of a movement making a real difference in business and beyond.

So, keep going, keep pushing for improvement, and most importantly, keep believing in the power of LPI to unlock the true potential of the organizations and people you work with. Your work matters, and the world needs more professionals like you to lead the way.

Chapter 6
What's on the Horizon: Absolute Value Online Solutions

As I look toward the future, I am excited to announce the launch of Absolute Value Online Solutions, a venture designed to harness my extensive experience in LPI and digital marketing to assist businesses in resolving operational challenges. This new platform represents a significant step forward in my journey to support organizations in their quest for continuous improvement. I am eager to share the vision and goals underpinning this initiative.

Absolute Value Online Solutions is highly focused on making LPI more accessible and practical for organizations across various industries . These practical implementations can help the firm succeed by adopting the changes required at that time. The ultimate goal of LPI is to provide the business with some effective solutions that can improve efficiency and productivity while ensuring that employees remain engaged and motivated. This approach knows that successful improvements should not come at the cost of employee well-being but should enhance the overall work environment.

The launch of Absolute Value Online Solutions has allowed me to share my passion for LPI and my years of experience in the field. The internet has revolutionized how knowledge and expertise are shared, making it possible to reach a broader audience and provide valuable support to those in need. Through this platform, I aim to democratize access to LPI principles and methodologies, allowing organizations of all sizes to benefit from proven techniques for improving their operations.

At Absolute Value Online Solutions, we offer personalized coaching to help organizations either embark on their LPI journey or recalibrate their existing efforts. This tailored approach ensures that each organization receives the specific guidance and support needed to address its unique challenges. Whether a company is just beginning to explore LPI or seeking to refine and optimize its current processes, we aim to provide practical, actionable advice that leads to sustainable improvements.

One of Absolute Value Online Solutions key features is its commitment to practical guidance. My experience has taught me that while theoretical knowledge is important, the real value comes from applying these principles in real-world scenarios. Our coaching sessions are designed to guide organizations along the correct path to beginning their LPI journey or helping those organizations that have started their LPI journey course correct to achieve LPI operating system integration marked by more sustained and impactful outcomes. We work closely with organizations to identify areas for improvement, develop strategies for LPI deployment and integration, as well as assist with the location of specialized on-site support providers if desired. At some point in the not-so-distant future, Absolute Value Online Solutions intends to harness the power of blockchain technology to support an LPI network that connects organizations in need of LPI support with experienced LPI professionals across the globe. In addition to the network community, the Absolute Value Online Solutions blockchain network intends to provide organizations access to a blockchain-based data acquisition system that can link disjointed legacy systems of record to provide accurate real-time operations data critical for quick operational performance assessment and implementation of effective countermeasures to address process efficiency and effectiveness issues.

In addition to offering LPI coaching, Absolute Value Online Solutions also provides resources for individuals interested in leveraging digital platforms for entrepreneurial ventures. The internet has opened up new opportunities for sharing skills, talents, and expertise with a global audience. For those looking to start their own digital businesses or expand their online presence, we offer guidance and resources to help turn these aspirations into reality. Whether you are a professional with a valuable skill set or someone with a passion for a particular field, our platform can assist you in navigating the digital landscape and building a successful online presence.

Creating Absolute Value Online Solutions has been a fulfilling endeavor, reflecting my commitment to helping organizations and individuals achieve their goals. By combining my knowledge of LPI with digital marketing strategies, I am able to offer a comprehensive range of services that address both operational and entrepreneurial needs. The platform represents a convergence of my professional experiences and personal passions, creating an innovative and impactful resource.

Looking ahead, I am excited about the opportunities that Absolute Value Online Solutions will create for businesses and individuals. The principles of LPI have the potential to transform organizations, and my mission is to ensure that these benefits are accessible to as many people as possible. Through personalized coaching, practical guidance, and digital resources, we aim to support continuous improvement and entrepreneurial success.

www.ingramcontent.com/pod-product-compliance
Lightning Source LLC
Chambersburg PA
CBHW070947220526
45471CB00007B/2929